ROSIE HAINE studied children's book illustration at the Cambridge School of Art, and she has also earned an MA in Globalization, Ethnicity, and Culture from Sussex University. Her research for this book included extensive reading, trips to caves, and conversations with an archaeologist. Her other books include *It Isn't Rude to Be Nude* and *Hooves or Hands?* (both Tate Publishing). Rosie lives in England. Visit her website at rosiehaine.co.uk and follow her on Instagram @futureisrosie.

Text and illustrations © 2023 Rosie Haine
Published by arrangement with Debbie Bibo Agency
Original book design by Orith Kolodny

First published in the United States in 2023
by Eerdmans Books for Young Readers,
an imprint of Wm. B. Eerdmans Publishing Co.
Grand Rapids, Michigan

www.eerdmans.com/youngreaders

Manufactured in the United States of America

31 30 29 28 27 26 25 24 23   1 2 3 4 5 6 7 8 9

ISBN 978-0-8028-5601-2

A catalog record of this book is available from the Library of Congress.

Illustrations created digitally with handmade textures

WE ARE HUMAN ANIMALS

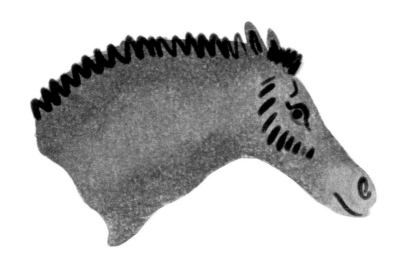

ROSIE HAINE

EERDMANS BOOKS FOR YOUNG READERS

GRAND RAPIDS, MICHIGAN

We are human animals.

We grew up in the wilds.

We got up with the sun
each day.

And went to sleep
when it got dark.

The seasons were
our calendar.

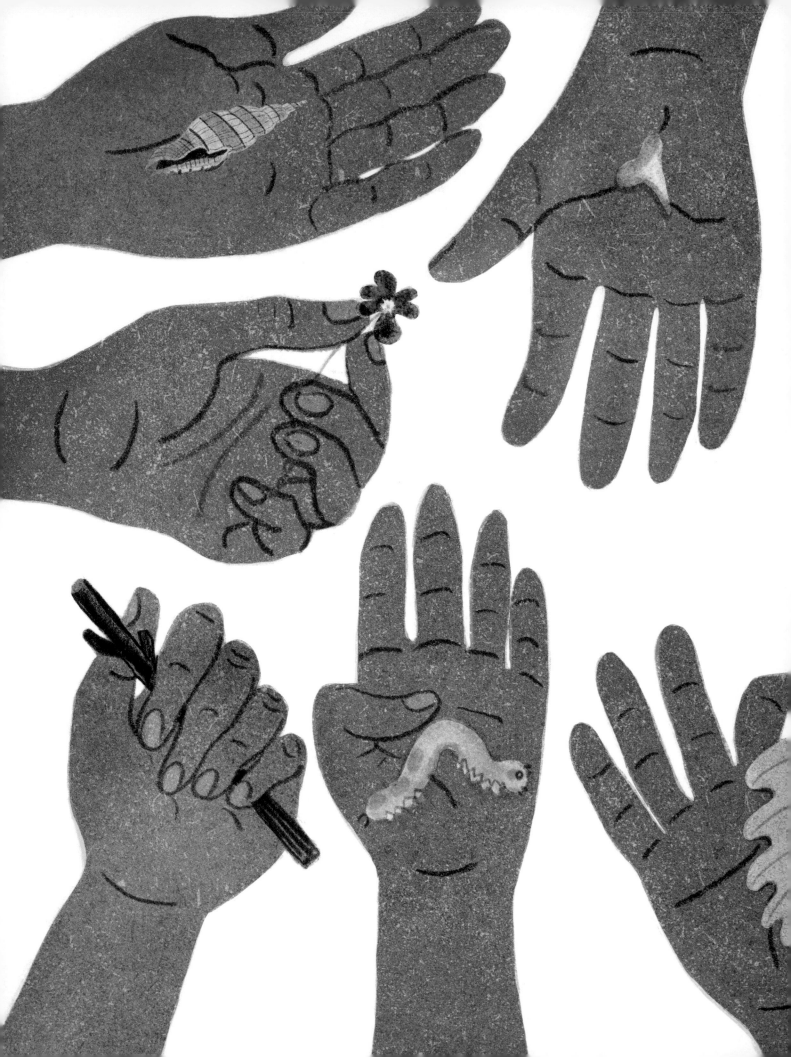

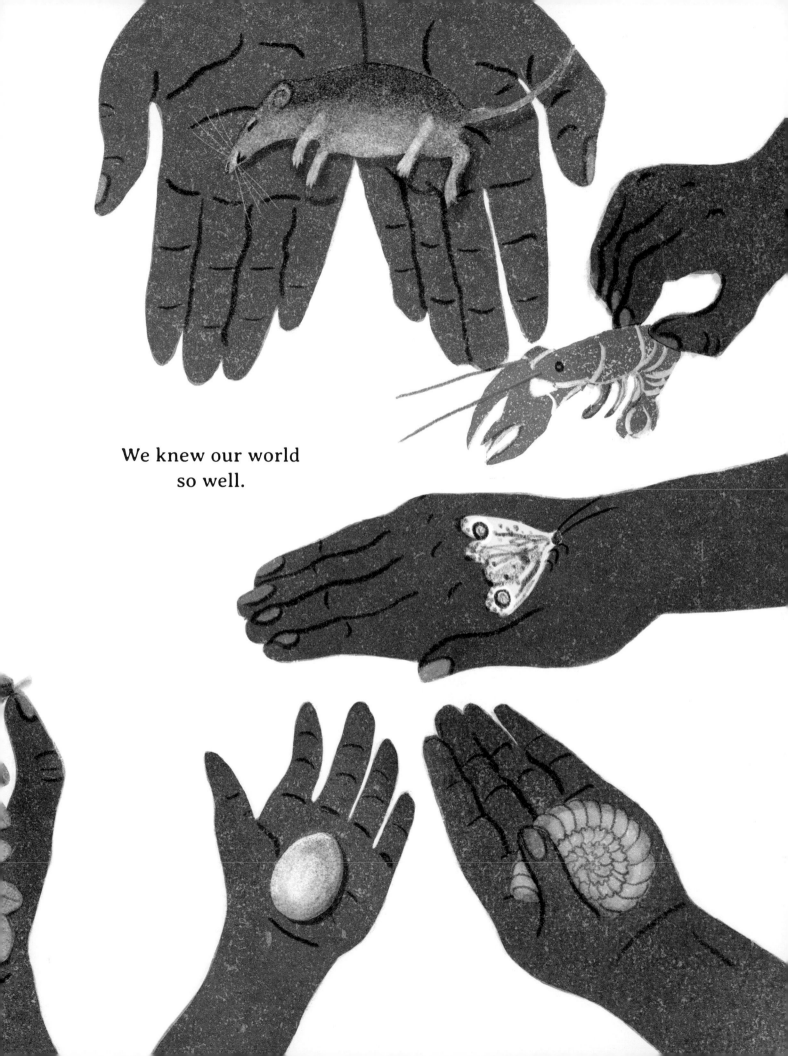

We knew our world
so well.

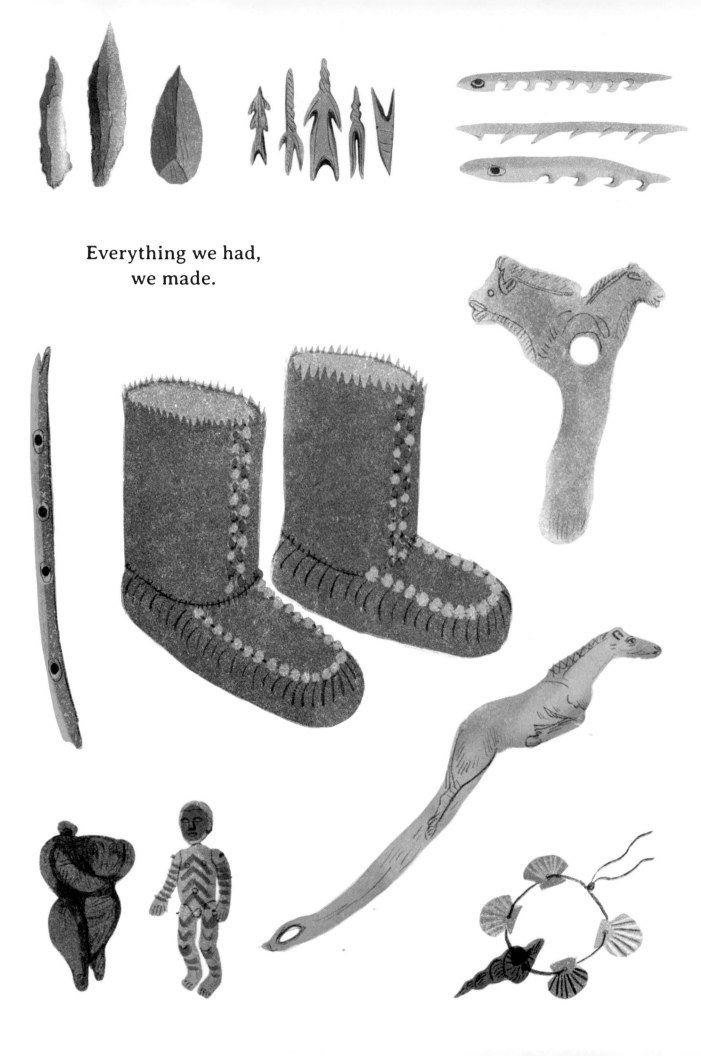

Everything we had,
we made.

Everything we ate, we picked or caught.

Some animals became
our friends.

Others were our food.

Some thought that we were their food!

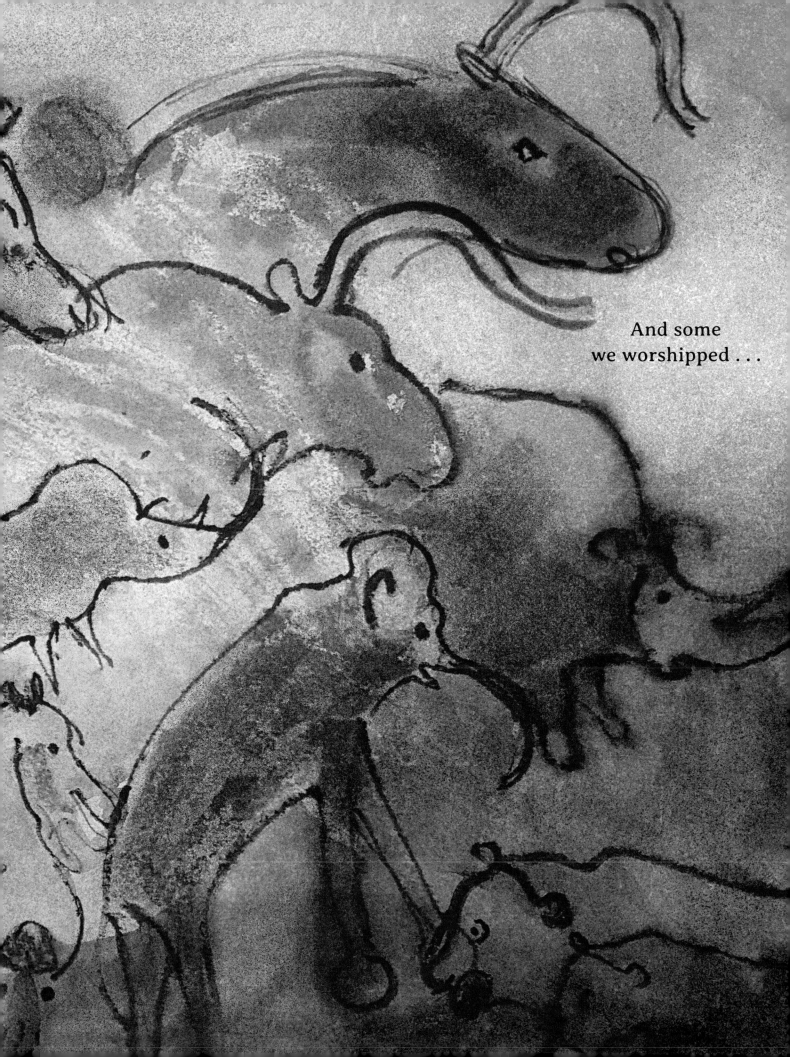

And some
we worshipped . . .

The sun and moon were
mysteries.

The stars,
our guiding
lights.

We played
music.

We had
clothes.

We wore
jewelry.

We made
art.

We made up
names for
all of it . . .

Every creature,
thought, and
flower.

We loved to meet,
to talk and dance,
and wonder at
our world.

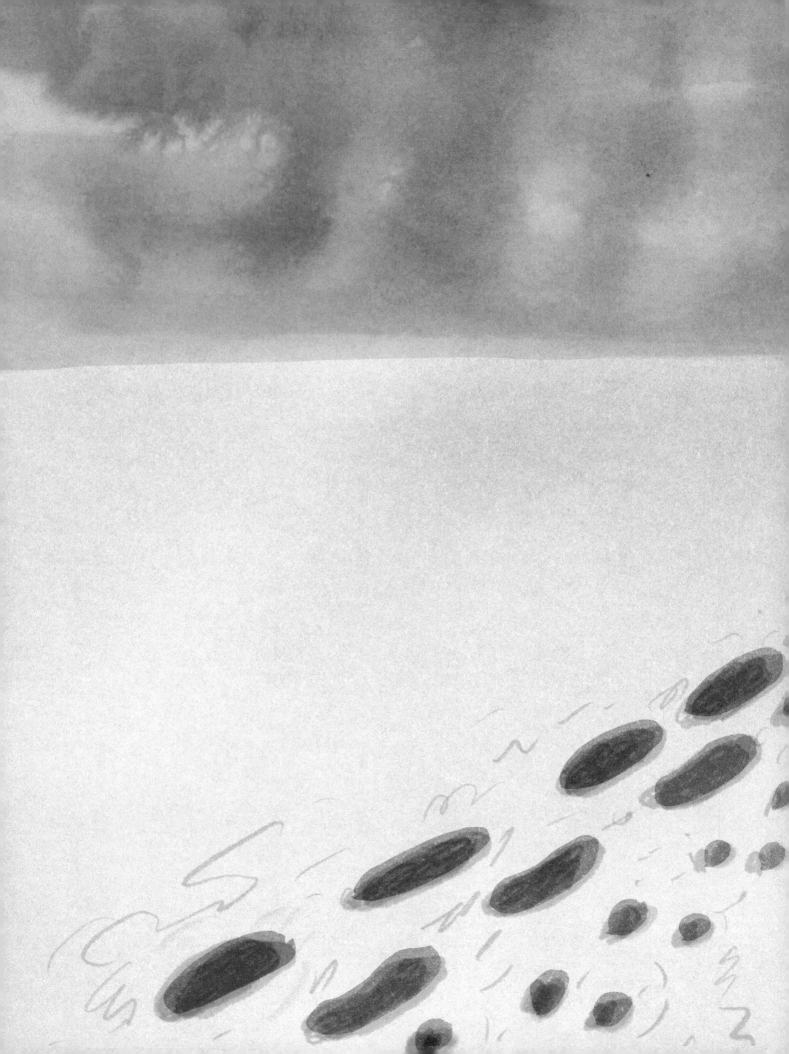

This was tens
of thousands of
years ago.

The world is very
different now,
but . . .

We are still
human animals.

AUTHOR'S NOTE

Many thousands of years ago, the first humans like us lived on earth—first in Africa, before moving to other continents as the world warmed up at the end of the last ice age. Our planet was very different then. Nature ruled, with huge animals like mammoths, giant wildebeest, and rhinoceroses roaming the earth in large numbers, migrating across continents in search of food. Humans were a minority: there were just millions then, but we now number in the billions. We lived nomadic lives, following the seasons and the animals that we relied upon for our food.

Some evidence from that time survives to this day. Wonderful cave paintings, carved objects, tools, and weapons have been found, giving us clues to imagine

our ancestors' lives. But so much of what they did and what they were like has been lost. What we do know is that humans lived as part of nature, and that much of what we did then has made us who we are now.

The family in this book are Upper Paleolithic hunter-gatherers, living in what is now France or nearby, about 25,000 years ago. These first European humans had dark skin and eyes, which we know because we have been able to sequence DNA from their remains. Even 10,000 years ago (centuries after this book's setting), Europeans had the skin-color genetic markers of people from sub-Saharan Africa. One of these people was Cheddar Man, whose fossilized bones were found in a cave in Cheddar Gorge, Somerset, England. While I was working on this book, I had a picture of what archaeologists think he looked like pinned to my studio wall.

Our Paleolithic ancestors made beautiful, stirring paintings like those in Chauvet, a cave in southeastern France that was only rediscovered in 1994, having been sealed by a landslide thousands of years ago. The paintings show horses, rhinos, hyenas, lions, and bison, drawn by artists who must have been so familiar with, and so in

Cheddar Man was one of the first people known to have blue eyes, a gene that had not yet developed at the time this book is set.

awe of these creatures. Chauvet's paintings—and the ones I viewed in other French caves like Pech Merle—inspired those in this book.

The paw prints of a wolf were also found in Chauvet. Was this an early domesticated wolf, on its way to becoming a dog?

Around the world, many museums contain examples of "portable" artworks from this period. They are small and light so they could be carried easily. I was inspired by the "Venus of Brassempouy," the head of a girl or young woman. Found in France, at about 25,000 years old, it is one of the oldest known realistic carvings of a human face.

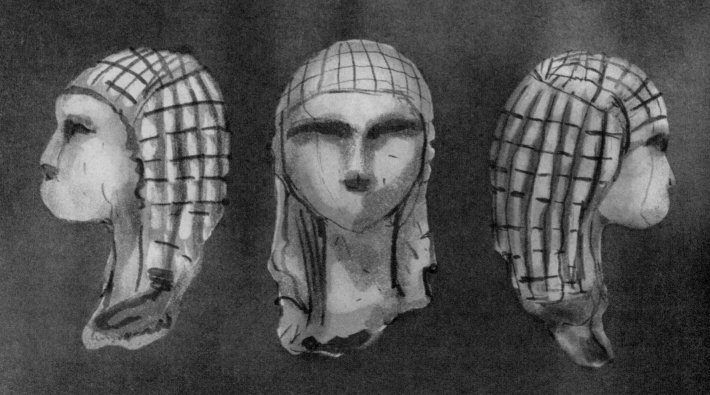

On the woman's head is what some have interpreted as a hood, wig, or a type of woven headdress. I think she is wearing her hair in braids, and this idea inspired the way the mother in this story wears her hair.

I often think about the lost world of our Paleolithic ancestors, and I feel as though I miss it. Despite the evidence we have of that time, there is still so much we don't know. And I think that the world was also mysterious to those early humans. What did our ancestors feel when a full moon—the same moon we gaze up at now—rose above a mountain?

Human nature comes from our place in nature—we may have airplanes, mobile phones, and space travel now, but our emotions, bodies, and minds were designed for this earlier time. Sometimes I sense a call from this forgotten part of my mind, a half-remembered instinct or understanding, and I know that I, too, am a human animal.

CLUES LEFT BEHIND...

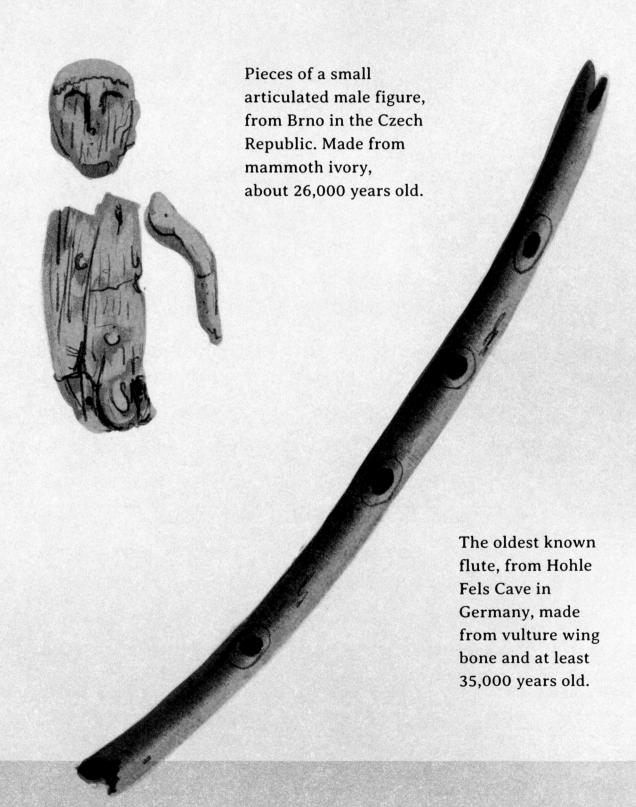

Pieces of a small articulated male figure, from Brno in the Czech Republic. Made from mammoth ivory, about 26,000 years old.

The oldest known flute, from Hohle Fels Cave in Germany, made from vulture wing bone and at least 35,000 years old.

The Venus of Hohle Fels,
found in Germany, mammoth
ivory, 35,000–40,000 years old.

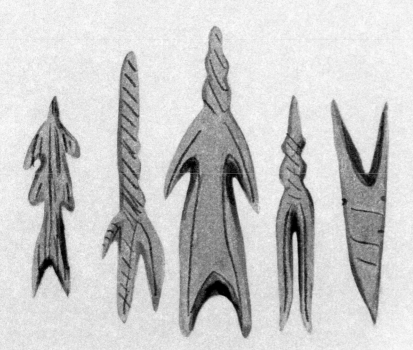

Fishhooks made
from antler, found in
Courbet Cave, France.
About 12,500 years old.

The Vogelherd Horse,
found in Germany,
mammoth ivory,
at least 35,000
years old.